THE MAGIC FORMULA
FOR PERSONAL POWER

10 STEPS IN SELF DEVELOPMENT

BY MIKHAIL STRABO

ISBN: 978-1-62504-053-4

www.myjaguarbooks.com
sales@myjaguarbooks.com

www.MyJaguarBooks.com

FOREWORD

There is a group of individuals that feel defenseless against destiny. They are those who sit and watch as things just happen; always feeling they have no control over them.

On the other hand, there are those who make things happen exactly the way they want.

This is called personal power.

This book, written by Mikhail Strabo clearly explains how you can transition from the first group and become like those who do not wait but rather take action to make things happen.

Developing personal power is a pathway to happiness. This means leaving behind things that do not work to start developing new habits that will bring you closer to your ideal status.

Nevertheless, be aware. Some people might think personal power and self discipline are the same. But we say self discipline is a tool. Personal power is an attitude in which you are always asking yourself "what if?", and are never afraid to test new waters or to overcome obstacles.

You will learn to change the voice in your head that puts you down and tells you: you can't. With this book you will remember: if you want to, you can. You will and can always accomplish the goals you set your mind on.

Strabo will take you, step by step, through a process in which you will awake your senses and your potentials to set a higher level of accomplishment in your life.

You will be able to establish goals and make them happen. In the modern era, Arte Moreno, an American businessman, owner of the Anaheim Angels, said: "A goal is a dream with a deadline."

Do not let a single thing stop you, especially yourself. This book will show you how to put a deadline in your dreams. Let yourself be guided by Strabo.

Bernabé Pérez, California, 2013

INTRODUCTION

THIS IS A BOOK FOR YOU.

You do not require a college degree or years of study at the feet of some master of esoteric lore to understand what I have to give you.

I have kept the secret, mystic and technical words, phrases and symbols out of my explanations.

The language I use is simple and easily understood. The ideas are given to you in the language you use and understand.

I have but one thing to suggest. When you first pick up this book, read it from beginning to end without trying to study or practice the methods I suggest. Just read it, so that you will know what is before you and so that you will not be curious about your future exercises.

Then, start from the beginning. Take one step at a time. Read one chapter at a time. Don't try to crowd too much into a few days. Don't set a schedule for yourself, so many days to a chapter or the like. Each step may take you a week, a month or a year. Some steps will be surmounted quicker than others. Don't go on to the next step until you have mastered the preceding step.

You will be able to tell when you are ready to go on with successive steps. You will distinctly know whether or not you are making progress. If you feel you have not yet completely mastered each successive exercise.

These simple declaratives are the markers of your progress. Keep them in your mind and on your tongue as you practice the examples in each step. Let them be the constant reminders of your sincerity. Repeat them to yourself, over and over. Let the meaning of these simple affirmations sink into your consciousness. Use them as a tonic when you feel the need. They can mean much to you. They will mean much to you if you are serious in your effort to attain Power.

They have meant much to me.

Mikhail Strabo, December 1943

WHAT IS POWER?

In order to give you a clear picture of what Power actually is, let me repeat an old story that you doubtless know.

There were five blind men who had heard someone speak of an elephant. Being curious, they started out in search of one of these remarkable animals.

After traveling for some time, they came to a place where an elephant was kept in captivity. The first blind man walked over and put his arms around one of the animal's huge legs.

"Aha," he said, "At last I know. The elephant is like a tree."

The second blind man learned against the beast's body and said, "No, you're wrong, the elephant is like a wall."

The third caught hold of the elephant's tail and cried. "You're both wrong, it's like a rope."

The fourth took hold of the animal's tusk and said, "No, the elephant is like a spear."

The fifth blind man grasped the beast's trunk and called out, "I'm sorry you're all wrong. The elephant is like a snake."

And so confusion reigned among the five blind men while they argued over their convictions.

This story is a perfect example of the meanings that different people give to Power. Power means something different to each individual. Particularly to the people who will read this book.

The very fact that you have begun reading this book proves that you are different from the general run of people. You are not content to remain as you are. You want to better yourself. You want the things in life that are rightfully yours. You, by your willingness to learn, have set yourself apart as one of the world's elect. Those who are prepared to dig deep in order to know the secret of the abundant life.

Therefore, you are different… or, at least, you aim to be different.

For that reason I know you will have your own definition of what Power means to you, individually.

That is as it should be, for we are all different. We look at life differently. We expect different things from life. But, like the five blind men, our definitions of life and Power are limited to that phase of life with which we are most familiar.

Too few of us are able to stand back and contemplate life in its various and different phases. It is in the development of this ability that our individual Power will grow to its greatest strength.

In order to help you attain this end, I will direct my words to you, individually. It will be as if we are talking together, one to the other. Then you will realize and understand that my words apply directly to you.

You, being an individual creation of the will of the Creator, have within yourself the beginnings of greatness. You have that touch of divinity that shines through your eyes. You have that spark of divine flame that lights up your consciousness. That is the never-dying Power within you that is constantly striving to make itself felt, seen and understood.

You have but to open the gates of your consciousness and Power will rise from you to become your ever-present servant.

NOTHING CAN STAND IN YOUR WAY.

NOTHING CAN HOLD YOU BACK.

YOUR WILL TO ATTAIN IS YOUR ONLY SURE WAY TO POWER.

Let us begin at the beginnings of life itself. You were brought into this life with a definite destiny to perform. The color of your hair may be different. Your skin may be light or dark. Your parents may or may not hold to one of the many different faiths or beliefs. All these things are unimportant.

The important thing is that you are individually the handiwork of the Master. Your station in life has been pre-ordained for you by Him. It is not a part of the divine plan that you should be submerged in your own unwillingness to attain. In His perfect plan you are marked for a definite position. That is your rightful place.

Whether you reach it or not depends upon how you make use of His divine guidance and His divine law.

The road you take and the way you progress is entirely in your own hands.

No one can hold you back. No one can keep you from attaining your goal. Only you can hold yourself back, only you can stand in your own way. And likewise, only you can help yourself.

To you as an individual, Power has a definite meaning. It may mean wealth, or health, or love, or strength, or knowledge, or the ability to influence others. I could continue through the list of human desires and in each instance it will represent the Power-aim of some individual.

But, no matter what your definition may be. No matter what name you give it, the way is the same. There are certain well defined laws that you must follow if you are to reach your Power-aim.

You have but to step out, to reach out, to grasp it and it will be yours forever.

To simplify our work, I have divided the way into ten logical steps. Ten steps that you can take one after the other in regular sequence. Ten steps that will open the gates of understanding and lead you to the glories of Power. Ten steps that will bring out the true you in all its divine glory and sublime Power.

From now on, your advancement is in your hands.

THE FIRST STEP

KNOW WHAT YOU WANT.

(I SEEK)

The most important thing in your life is to know what you want.

It is in the knowing that the victory is half won.

There is nothing so helpless as a rudderless ship in a gale. It goes in all directions with each succeeding wave and wind.

So it is with the individual who has no definite aim in life. He goes here and there, to this side and then to that, backwards and forwards. Spending his precious energy, his still more precious time and wasting the precious matter of his ambition.

The white mouse in the whirling cage covers a lot of ground but ends up exactly where he started.

Look at the lives of the people whom you know who have attained their Power-aim in life.

Starting out with a definite aim, they made their plans and stuck to them. They knew at all times exactly where they were going. They kept their eyes on their goal at all times. They let nothing stand in their way. Whenever an obstacle appeared in their path they found some way to climb over it, get around it or tunnel underneath it. There may have been some slight delays, but there was no stopping. They were on their way to a definite goal. They were determined that nothing would stand in their way.

This is your first step.

SELECT YOUR GOAL.

Decide what you want Power to mean for you.

This is not done by merely attempting to copy somebody else. You do not write several goals on several pieces of paper, drop them into a hat, and then pick one of them out blindfolded, and proclaim it to the world as your specific Power aim.

Of course, that is the fool's way.

There is a true way to find your Power-aim. A sure way.

Go into the silence. There all things are made clear and understandable. Sit down quietly, by yourself. Concentrate on the things that you want Power to mean to you.

Don't believe that you can think this problem out in a few minutes.

IT WILL BE THE MOST IMPORTANT DECISION IN YOUR LIFE.

Give it time, plenty of time.

Give it thought, plenty of thought.

Sit in a semi-darkened room, where there I nothing to distract you.

Get yourself comfortable. Do not fidget. Do not strain. Sit at ease. Do not think of anything at all. Empty your mind of all thoughts, as you would empty a waste basket. Do not stare at any one spot on the wall or in the room. Relax, Relax, Relax.

Thoughts will come into your mind. Strange thoughts. Do not make an effort to drive them out. You will find yourself thinking of many things. Don't try too hard to remember any of these thoughts.

Sit quietly for about fifteen minutes. Don't hold a watch on yourself. If you do not get an answer the first time you sit in the silence, don't be disappointed.

Continue your silent meditations day after day, preferably in the morning before you begin your day's work. While you are fresh and alert. While there is not much noise about to distract you.

Try to do this at the same time each morning.

After a few days of morning silences, repeat these periods in the evening, before you go to sleep. In this way you will go into a regular program of morning and evening silence periods.

At first you may find it difficult to sit quietly and clear your mind, but as you continue practicing you will find great comfort and help in this daily exercise.

(For those of my readers who are interested in knowing more of this form of concentration and development, I suggest that they read my book **The Magic Formula For Successful Prayer.** There, they will find a more detailed explanation of the technique of attaining this personal Power medium).

Eventually you will receive a message... a suggestion... a cue to that which you are seeking.

You may call it hunch, but that may be your sign. That may be the indication for which you are seeking.

Be sure that the goal you select is one that is within your reach. Don't try for something for which you are manifestly unprepared. But, since you are practically unprepared for any goal, you must be reconciled to the fact that attainment is to be filled with much effort and much work.

How often have we heard the old adage, Anything that is worth having is worth working for. How true that is when it concerns your Power-aim.

Once you know what you want, point every energy towards it. Keep your goal in mind 24 hours each day.

Don't change your Power-aim with every new thought or with every new mind. Don't envy another. Don't try to copy other people. Remember you are an individual and you are on your way to Power.

At this time it is best to give you a word of warning. It is in regard to interpreting messages or hunches.

Don't think that as you sit in silence a blackboard will appear before you and a supernatural hand will write a message for you to read and remember. Your message and your answers will come in various ways.

It may come to you as a vision in the silence. A vision that is so clear and detailed that you cannot mistake it. It may come in other ways. You may get a hunch to go to a certain place, where something will happen. That may be your message. It may come as a suggestion to call upon someone where some suggestions might lead you onward.

Your message will come in many strange and devious ways. Ways that may seem strange and unrelated. It is not your province to ask why or how. You must be ready for them when they come. You must accept that it is the way in which the Master is working out his answer for you.

I remember a man coming to see me complaining that his sessions in the silence had been unproductive of results. He told me how he had faithfully sat and communed with the Master but there were no results.

He then proceeded to tell me how he had just obtained a new position. How he happened to be walking along a certain street, one that he rarely had occasion to frequent. There he met a friend quite unexpectedly and how this friend had told him about a certain position that was open. He went to that place immediately and now the position was his, and it was a good position at that.

I asked him why he happened to go down that street. And the answer surprised him, but it didn't surprise me, for I knew what the answer would be.

He told me that after he finished his regular morning silence session he felt impelled to walk downtown. Instead to take him down the other and there he met a friend.

I told him that he had indeed been fortunate that his hunch had pushed him into the street where his destiny was waiting for him in the shape of his friend.

It was then, without a suggestion on my part, that he realized that his sessions with the Master had not been in vain.

You may come face to face with the same problem. You may not seem to get a message through to you don't despair. Don't give yourself another week or another month to wait for the answer. Don't use a calendar or a clock on your contacts with the Master. This attitude may be the obstacle that you create.

KEEP YOUR MIND EVERLASTINGLY ON YOUR GOAL.

I could tell you the stories of hundreds of people who reached their Power-aim. But this book is about you. Your problem is your own. What others have done in the past is of no interest to you at this moment.

Now you are starting out on your own journey. Your mind must be clear.

You are and always should be the most important person in the world to yourself.

You have only 24 hours each day to use in the quest of your Power-aim. Use the wisely.

If something should come into your life that may distract or take you from the continuation of your own personal quest, think twice before you waste any of your precious hours in the pursuit of a will-of-the-wisp.

Remember the story of the Hare and the Tortoise. How the Tortoise won the race because he plodded on, kept his eyes on the goal and did not stop to rest or chase flies. The Hare, with victory in his grasp, lay down by the side of the road for a nap. That's how he lost the race.

Rather emulate the Tortoise than the Hare. There are a great number of people who star off on a job with speed and enthusiasm. Unfortunately, they tire easily and must lie down to rest. Those who work along steadily and steadfastly are the ones who will reach the goal first. They are the winners.

They may not be as brilliant or as dashing as the speeders, but their attainments are the more lasting. They have learned the lesson of sticking to it until victory is won.

The race is not always to the swift.

The race is always to the one who knows where he is going. To the one who keeps his eye and his heart on Victory.

As you take your first step towards your Power-aim, think well of your objective.

KNOW WHAT YOU WANT.

KNOW WHERE YOU ARE GOING.

Keep your eyes, your mind, your heart, all your thoughts and all your energies on your goal.

Think it, live it, act it, breathe it all the time.

Once you have mastered this, once you know where you are going, once you have learned to concentrate on your objective, then, and only then are you ready for the next step.

THE SECOND STEP

THE CONQUEST OF FEAR

(I TRUST)

You may ask the question, "What has fear to do with the quest for personal Power?"

You must understand that fear is the bogey that stalks the steps of most people and keeps them from a complete development of their own individual personality.

Fear is mortal man's greatest enemy.

It may be the fear of the future, fear of failure, fear of another, fear of one's own self, fear of the hereafter or any of the thousand and one fears that follow people through life.

There are a great many things that we have come to call by other names that have their root in fear.

Take envy. Envy is one of the many manifestations of fear. When we are envious of others we really fear them. If we would be honest with ourselves and analyze our actions and reactions we would be able to give our acts their proper names. Think it over. You'll agree with me.

A great many people fear to be alone. Not that they are frightened by the dark or the possibility of someone lurking in their path.

They are afraid to be with themselves. They are afraid of their own thoughts. They are afraid of themselves. That may be the source of that familiar quotation of being afraid of one's shadow.

Ages ago, a wise man said, "Know thyself and thou wilt know all things."

Knowing one's self is more than the mere knowledge that you have a scar on your left elbow, or that your right shoulder is higher than your left shoulder.

It is knowing your mind, knowing your abilities, understanding your reac tions.

Knowing yourself is the end of all fears.

You may fear to start on this path to your Power-aim because of one of several reasons. You may fear you will not be able to understand the instructions. You may fear you will not be able to keep your mind on your plans. You may fear that it will take too much time from your usual diversions, or any one of a dozen other fears.

You may fear the ridicule of others who believe themselves too wise to try to improve themselves. It is well to remember that people of that type of thinking are subject to their own private fears.

AND NOW... A WARNING;

(If you have definitely decided upon your personal Power-aim, keep it to yourself. Don't go about discussing it with others. Don't look upon it as a subject for boasting. No one can help you but yourself. Other people can only hinder you. They can only burden you with their help. Other people, who think they know more than you do, can only make your way more difficult by their suggestions. You are an individual. You are seeking a way that from the beginning, you will be saved from the for yourself. Don't try to help others until you have learned how to help yourself. Don't take too much of a load at the beginning. Remember, you must learn to creep before you can walk, and you must feel your way before you can run. You are an individual. Remain an individual.)

You do not banish fears by forgetting about them. That is dangerous. You must bring your fears out in the open. Know them. Recognize them when they appear. Realize that fear is but a human frailty and it will disappear.

Worries are a form of fear. You fear the worst. But once you know the worst, it ceases to exist, and you are free from fear.

Never worry about anything that you feel is about to happen. It never does happen. If you understand that fear preys on the mind of the person who expects the worst.

Worry is a disease. A disease that can be cured. A disease that ceases to exist the moment the cause is brought out in the light of understanding.

If you have learned the lessons of the preceding step, you will know the sure way of getting rid of your cares, real and imaginary.

Your refuge and your answer is in the silence. There, in your daily communications with the Master, you can unburden yourself of all the thoughts and fears that trouble and vex you.

Always keep this thought before you.

THERE IS NO POWER THAT CAN HARM YOU.

No power outside of yourself. You are the only person that you have to fear.

But, if understanding is born within you. If you realize that you possess a Power that can overcome all obstacles, if you realize that your mind is all-Powerful and all embracing, if you accept these things, then you are beyond all fear.

It is only your shortcomings that can harm you. Envy, hate, pity, greed, laziness, pride, boastfulness, anger, lust . . . these are the things you must avoid or overcome if you will be without fear.

Practice a regular avoidance of all these weaknesses. Don't think you can overcome them in a single session in the silence. Some of these fears may, through years of weakness or ignorance, have become an integral part of your thinking. You cannot expect to completely change yourself in a day, or a week, or a month, or even a year.

You must apply yourself. Check yourself carefully. Go over the things that you have done each day. Be your own prompter. Check up on yourself. No one else can check you on the things you do each day. You can, at least, be honest with yourself. You will know when you have over-stepped one of the danger lines, and knowing, you will best be able to correct yourself.

Here's a suggestion for you. Try it on yourself for a few days and watch the results.

Prepare a little paper. List all these shortcomings on it. Then, as you go through your daily life, watch yourself. Whenever you cross one of the danger lines place a mark alongside the weakness to which you have succumbed.

Then, analyze your behavior. If you are honest with yourself, if you keep a close watch on your actions, you will be able to curb yourself.

It is through the conquest of these short comings that you will learn self-control. It is through self-control that you will be able to conquer fear.

Once fear no longer has a place in your life, in your thinking, in your actions, you will be free to go on to the greater accomplishments. You will have unburdened yourself. There will be nothing to hold you back.

Each of the shortcomings that I have enumerated is but another manifestation of fear. Think them out and you will understand exactly what I mean. I will not take time or space here to go into the psychological aspects of this association. You are an intelligent person. You have a mind that you are training to think logically. You are training your mind to be your servant so that it will help you reach your personal Power-aim. Here is some work for it.

Do not be suspicious of others. Either their actions, their motives or their words. Remember that no one can harm you. No one can take anything from you. Your wealth is in your being. It is only when you permit yourself to be brought down to another's level that you are taking something from yourself. Only then will you lose some of that wealth that should be yours forever.

You can fool the world, but you cannot fool yourself. When you sit alone in the silence, when you are naked before your Master, when you honestly review the things you did the day before, then you must be honest with yourself.

Don't try to find excuses for yourself. Don't try to figure out reasons why you did this or why you neglected to do that. The weak man and the coward can always justify a weakness or a fear.

THERE IS NO SUCH THING AS A FEAR.

Fear is something that you yourself create. The things that you create, you can dispel. Fear is a name that you give to a situation that you dare not face.

Repeat the following words over and over to yourself.

I SHALL FEAR NO EVIL FOR THOU ART WITH ME.

Should a moment of weakness come over you. Should you feel yourself about to fail, repeat those words, over and over again. Mean them. Think them. Feel them.

You will experience a feeling of strength of Power, of confidence come over you.

YOU WILL BE FREE.

THE THIRD STEP

THE GROWTH OF CONFIDENCE

(I REACH)

After you know what you want, and you are definite about it, and after you have put all fear behind you, then you will step into a new phase of life.

A phase that has much to do with your own development. A phase that will do much to carry you forward to your Power-aim.

You will feel a confidence surging within you. You will feel a glorious Power within you. You will have supreme faith in yourself.

Knowing that you have complete control of your thinking you will recognize the Power that is to give your self-confidence a solid foundation.

You are now an INDIVIDUAL. Your thinking is straight and true. You are honest in your self-analysis. You are consciously correcting your faults. You have learned to bear with other people. You are no longer lonesome or alone. Your thoughts are with you at all times. They are helping you in every step you take along your path.

You no longer fear the truth. You understand that the truth is your rightful heritage. The truth has now become an integral part of your daily life. You are the truth, and the truth is you.

You can now face the world, knowing that you fear no man.

From now on you will be the pure manifestation of your thoughts. You will be what you think you are. You will think health and you will be healthy. You will think beauty and you will be beautiful. You will think of the Master's unlimited supply and it will be yours to use wisely. You will think love to all the world and love will come into your life. You will, at all times, be the result of your thinking.

In your daily work, in your contacts with others, in your own silent sessions with the Master, you will find yourself growing to a new stature.

The problems that had heretofore seemed insurmountable will have dissolved. They will have ceased to exist.

Your thinking and the divine truth will be your constant protection.

You will be like a new-born child, learning to walk, learning to walk your own way, alone, unafraid, confident.

People will appear before you in their true proportions and their honest importance. Those whom you deemed great will now assume their human stature with all their human weaknesses and frailties clear to your eye.

Those who seemed to fill you with fear and dread will no longer cause you to tremble. The liar, the fraud and the cheat will not be able to fool you for Truth being on your side will protect you by revealing itself to you.

The thief can take nothing from you for your treasure will be in your confidence, in your faith in yourself.

The future will have no terrors for you, for now you know that the feature can only bring you greater confidence, greater Power, greater understanding.

Now you will stand on your own feet. You will look to no one but the Master for help. You will know that your help comes from within. It will come from the Power that you have created within yourself.

Tomorrow will no longer be a day to look forward to with dread and fear. You will look to all your tomorrows with confidence. Tomorrow will mean another opportunity for you to exercise your new strength.

Yesterday will be a book that you will study in order to find new ways to improve yourself.

Today will be yours forever. To do with as you know to be right. Each morning and each evening as you appear before yourself, in the Power building sessions of the silence, you will say over and over again until it is a part of your being.

"I AM THE PERFECT CHILD OF THE MASTER. I LIVE PERFECTION, I THINK PERFECTION, I AM PERFECTION. EACH NEW DAY, EACH NEW HOUR OFFERS ME NEW OPPORTUNITIES FOR THE PERFECT EXPRESSION OF MY PERFECTION."

Repeat this over and over. You will find the word guiding you to the perfect state that is your Power-aim.

THE FOURTH STEP

YOUR WILL TAKES OVER

(I WILL)

Once your confidence is firmly rooted in the ground that you have so faithfully cultivated, you will be ready to go on to the next step.

Now, YOUR WILL TAKES OVER, and you begin to feel and experience the fruits of your earlier application.

Instead of playing a passive role, your WILL takes an active part in all the things you do. You call on your Will on all occasions and your WILL responds. You climb to new heights, New vistas unfold themselves before your eager eyes. A new world opens to you. THE WORLD OF WILL.

I have found that most of the people who live on this earth aspire to something or other at various times in their lives. This goal may be Money, Power, Position, Influence, Health or any of the ends towards which man aspires. Yet, despite their very best intentions they never seem to attain their desires. Why?

There is but one answer. These people are not sufficiently definite about their goal, if they have a goal at all. They do not live their aspirations twenty-four hours a day. There are far too many unconnected interested that come between them and their Power-aim.

They are very much like the child in front of a Christmas tree. There are so many packages, so many glistering trinkets hanging from the tree that the youngster cannot concentrate his interest on any one thing.

These people are like the man who starved in the midst of plenty because he could not make up his mind which of the tempting morsels he should eat.

So you, who cannot bring yourself to that state where you can keep your eyes and your mind in one direction long enough to make that direction yours, will find that your goal, your aspiration, your Power-aim will escape you. It will slip through your fingers like the sand.

To wish for something is not enough. To feel that you should have what you are after is not enough. To hope for your goal is not enough. To dream of your Power-aim is not enough. YOU MUST WILL IT, actively at all times.

When your Will takes over, when it takes complete charge of your every action, when it assumes complete control of your every thought, then, and not until then, will you be on the road to your goal.

Your Will can exert a power greater than any that Man-made machinery can exert.

Your faith can move mountains. If you believe a thing with all the Will at your command, that thing is so, simply because you Will it. Nothing can stand in the way of your Will if you know how to control it.

It is in the sessions of the silence that you can gather up thin tremendous Power of your Will. You can store it up for the future, just as you store coal for the winter. Store up your extra supply of Will for the work of the day that is before you.

You can have an unlimited supply. You can have an unending supply. A supply that is only limited by your own willingness to admit that there is a limit to it. If you know and feel and understand that this unlimited Power that comes from within can take you wherever you aim to go. You can go wherever you Will. You can do whatever you Will. You can attain whatever you Will.

This silence, where you store up your supply of Will, must never be negative. It must not be a resting period. It must not be a period of day dreaming, of idle wishing. It must be positive, dynamic, alive.

YOU MUST MAKE IT A POSITIVE PERIOD.

You must by the exercise of your self control, by your ability to recognize the Word when it comes to you, make of this regular communication with your inner self and with the Master a period in which you make your plans to conquer your world.

Undirected Will takes the line of least resistance. It takes the easy way. Just as a brook winds its way around boulders and through gullies, your undirected Will finds it much easier to go around obstacles than it would be to overcome them.

Remember a dead fish floats with the current, it takes a live one to swim against the tide.

Build up your Will until you reach that stage in life when each new obstacle is welcomed as an opportunity to exercise your new-found Power.

Then when you have yourself well in hand. When you know where you are going. When you begin to recognize the new found strength that stems from within you. When your eye and your mind and your heart are centered on the goal that is yours, then... you are ready for the next step.

THE FIFTH STEP

YOU DARE TO TRY

(I CAN)

Like a child learning to walk alone, you step out, cautiously at first, to test the strength and extent of your new-found Power. As you discover that you can now do some of the things you previously had merely hoped to do, you experience the beginning of courage.

Now you are having your first demonstration of your new-found Power.

This is not the end. It's but the beginning. You still have quite a distance to go.

Now you build your goal carefully. Stone on Stone. You become the architect of your own destiny. You draw the plans of your Power-aim with all its details.

You already built the foundations in your earlier exercises, now you must be ready to go ahead. To stand still is to go back.

In life nothing stands still. It either moves forward or it moves backward. With your goal before you, you MUST move ahead, towards it. Any neglect, delay or temporary halt is a backward step.

Plan your edifice with your ideals. Make your Will the corner-stone of your building, for with the true exercise of your Will you become the embodiment of your ideals.

Your thoughts should be high; as high as you can aspire. You must at all times remember that you can be what you think you are.

The higher your thoughts, your ideals, your Power-aim, the higher will be the goal you will finally reach.

Fresh from a session with your Master in the silence you will find yourself looking upon the world with a new found courage. You look upon the world that meets you with different eyes, with deeper understanding.

You know where you are going. The aimless intentions of the rest of the world are apparent to you and you avoid them.

You are now an individual with a definite aim. You have an appointment with destiny. You are now on your way to your Power-aim.

You feel the new-born strength of your intentions. You learn the most important lesson that life has to teach you.

You learn that this tremendous Power-energy that is now a part of everything you feel, think or do is something that works through you. You are the medium through which it expresses itself.

You learn to repeat the litany of your faith.

I, OF MYSELF, DO NOTHING, THE POWER WITHIN ME DOES ALL THINGS.

You repeat this over and over again, until the true meaning of the words are revealed to you. They are revealed to you not in the static sense, as words alone, but in their active sense of Power working through you.

Words have a way of working for you. Your faith and your belief give them an intensity that is overwhelming. They are at once a challenge and an obligation.

A challenge to attain and the obligation to be true to yourself, your thinking and your faith.

Tomorrow no longer holds terrors for you. Your work, be it what it may, takes on a new proportion, assumes a new importance. Heretofore it was merely a means to an end. It meant food, clothing and shelter. Now it is something quite different. It is no longer a necessary social obligation alone.

Your work becomes an opportunity to serve. An opportunity to help those around you. An opportunity for you to grow in importance, in understanding and in accomplishment.

You are above jealously and envy, for now you realize that these are the emotions that would hold you back. They would keep you from your Power-aim. They are typical fear manifestations that you have learned to overcome in the early stages of your education.

The spite or envy of others can no longer harm you. You are impervious to all their barbs. You rise above the petty people and events. You are now the master of your own intentions. You are now ruler of your own thoughts. You are now the dictator of your own actions.

Your mind takes on New Power. It seems through the shams of life. It intuitively understands and anticipates the intentions of others. You are far beyond the heavy load of circumstances. You now create your own circumstances. You have risen above the crowd.

And all because you have learned the real meaning of the words you say. Because of your understanding. Because you have learned how to accept the help that is always ready for you.

Because they are no longer mere words, but your testament of faith. Each time you repeat them you strengthen your faith in your approach to your Power-aim.

I, OF MYSELF, DO NOTHING, THE POWER WITHIN ME DOES ALL THINGS.

THE SIXTH STEP

YOU STAND ON YOUR OWN FEET

(I MUST)

By this time, if you have been continuing your exercises in the silence with fidelity, you should be able to achieve demonstrations of your own.

You are no longer wishing, hoping or dreaming of everything that comes into my mind. You are definitely concentrating all your Will on the one goal that you have already so carefully selected.

You will find that your daily work, if you conduct it with sincerity, will be another way of reaching upwards and onwards towards your Power-aim.

A great many people feel that unless their work has some glamour or some seemingly interesting feature it is just something that takes up the time of the day. That it is merely a means of obtaining the necessities of life. They do just what is expected of them or as little as they possibly can without being discharged from their position. They feel that they are fooling the boss. They are not doing all the things that he expects them to do. They are fools. They believe that they are cleverer than others.

Unfortunately these people are merely fooling themselves. They are losing their greatest opportunity to practice for the days when their work will be entirely the work of their own Power-aim.

You should bear in mind every job you do, no matter how small or menial it may be, is always another test, another trial and another opportunity to grow and become proficient in the exercise of your own Will.

You, like many others, may not feel that your superior is treating you with the consideration that you deserve. You may feel that he is favoring others, that he does not recognize your importance, your seriousness, your application or your efforts.

All these occasions are just additional opportunities for you. An opportunity to show yourself that you can do what is right, that you can do as much as is required of you, and that you can do it intelligently. You don't have to try to prove it to your superior. Just prove it to yourself. Remember that you are the most important person in your own life. You are the one that must be satisfied with your own progress. You are the moss at all times. You are the person who sets the tune.

Some of your short-sighted fellow workers may try to undermine you. They may circulate false stories about you. They may try to lower you in the eyes of your superiors. Pay no heed to them. They cannot harm you. You are above them, for your protection is much stronger than the calumnies of others. You are divinely protected, for your store of faith built up during your sessions in the silent is stronger than any steel armor that you can wear.

These people do themselves far more harm than they can ever do you. Their envy, their jealously, their spite merely builds up their own inferiority. They are merely adding to their store of fear.

A person is merely the extension of his thoughts. You are what you think. If you think Power at all times you will exert Power. If you think hate, you will merely build up your own store of hate.

Be one who at all times radiates love, friendship, confidence and helpfulness.

You will soon impress those who come in contact with you. You will know how to use the Power of your thoughts. People around you will be quick to sense the beauty and the peace that constantly surround you. They will hesitate before they try to undermine you, for they will soon realize that they cannot harm you, that you are above all the patty thoughts and deeds that are a part of their lives.

Think back to the days when you disliked people. The more people you disliked, the more reason there was to dislike them and others. You were creating a source of that was able to generate nothing but hate.

Therefore keep your thoughts clean of all petty things. Do not fill your mind and your thinking with disagreeable thoughts. They multiply so quickly that you soon find yourself overwhelmed by thoughts that will hold you back from the attainment of your Power-aim.

In this way you will become a leader, one who will inspire others, one who will show the way to the weaklings.

The person who is always looking for a fight or an argument is not a person of Power. He is the embodiment of weakness. His belligerence is the only means that he has proven to himself that he is not a coward or a fool. The great tragedy of his life comes when he meets someone who is either stronger or can speak louder. His is a false strength, and a false confidence.

But the strength which is built on the solid foundation of your perfect understanding of your Power can never be destroyed or weakened.

Your confidence in yourself has the strength of a stone wall that cannot be battered down. For you, understanding the sources of your strength can keep renewing it from time to time. You can always, at any time, at any place and under any circumstances call upon the source of your Power and add to the directness and the definiteness of your aim.

This is the Power that can never be shaken. That is the Glory that can never be dimmed.

With this Power at your command you can stand on your feet. You can look into the eyes of the world unafraid. You can do the things that man had never done before.

The affirmation that you use at this stage of your progress is a simple one. One that embodies the story of your growth, the heart of your message and the soul of your Power.

THE POWER OF THE MASTER, MANIFESTED THROUGH ME, GIVES ME MY SHARE OF LIFE'S ABUNDANCE.

THE SEVENTH STEP

YOU REACH OUT

(I DO)

With this step you come to that stage in your progress where your Will is constantly directing you in all the things you undertake. With your newly developed sense of understanding you know that you are being divinely guided.

Each morning as you sit in the silence you discover that your day's instructions are being made understandable to you.

This may sound strange to you on the first reading, but it is so.

In the silence, your mind being at rest, your thoughts concentrated on your regular meeting with the Master, you will find thoughts coming and going through your mind.

Let them come and go. That is the way to clear your mind for the real message.

Your self-training will have taught you to recognize thoughts that come direct from your Power-source and separate them from those thoughts that come from your weak wish-bone.

Ideas will crystalize in your consciousness. You will get what many people call "hunches". There so called hunches are very often messages, instructions that you must follow.

In the silence the things that you had hitherto never understood will make themselves clear to you. You will see and understand the true reason for things, events and thoughts. You will begin to understand the manner in which the Master works out your destiny in his own way.

You are no longer in the dark, but in Life's most revealing and brightest light. You are the center of your universe. Into you now pours the Power to continue onward and upward, and in turn, from you will radiate all your good thoughts for others, all your good intentions, all the concentrated glory of your Mater source.

The thoughts that come to you in the silence are messages that are meant exclusively for you, and for no other. They are the guide posts that will show you the way ahead. They are the instructions that the Master mind has created and issued just for you.

You reach out for these messages and take them to yourself. They are your way.

Don't let them pass unnoticed. Make it your business to understand them clearly. You will be able to recognize how the fit into the pattern of your individual Power-aim. You will see the reason for them.

You reach out and take them to you. You reach out and follow these instructions. You reach out and encompass in your embrace the Will of the Master.

By following your instructions you will notice how much further ahead you go, how much faster you progress, and how much greater becomes your strength.

The unknowing, around you, will call your advancement and your accomplishments a miracle. But you, knowing and understanding from when it comes, will be glad to give it its correct name, which is progress.

Your progress will depend on how well you follow your instructions, how sincere you are in the application of the basic laws and how seriously you apply your concentrated Will on the attainment of your goal.

Keep your work to yourself. Don't discuss it with others. Discussing it with others is a sign of your lack of faith in yourself. It is a sign of weakness. It is a sign that you are seeking commendation from those whom you have tried to impress with your ambition. It's a sign of vanity.

Your work, your ambitions, your Power-aim is a matter that concerns but you and the Master. Go to him with your problems. Go to him with your questions. Then you are assured that they will be answered quickly and correctly.

Do not rely on mere man's judgment when you have the judgment of the All-Wise at your command.

The more often you call on the Master for help and advice. The more you will be able to stand on your own feet and the grater will be your Power. For the guiding spirit of the Will within you becomes more potent with use.

The more you use your Will the stronger it becomes.

You will find that the more you reach out for, the more you will accomplish. Your accomplishments will be limited only by your Will to attain.

Do not limit yourself. Do not draw an imaginary line and say to yourself, "So far I will go and no further."

Do not even think the words, for the very thought itself will limit your Power of accomplishment.

Realize that there is no limit to your own strength when it is copied with the strength of the Masters. There can be no limit to your Power when it is one with the Power source.

No outside influence can limit you. Limitation can only come from within yourself. You are the only person who can defeat your own aims.

You can therefore see the importance of your self-confidence, the necessity of your self-development and the need for your complete and undivided faith.

Always be ready to meet your problems face to face, with the Master at your side and call upon Him at all times for your guidance, support and strength.

Keep on repeating the words endlessly and meaningfully:

I, OF MYSELF, DO NOTHING, THE MASTER, WORKING HIS WILL THROUGH ME, DOES ALL.

THE EIGHTH STEP

UNDERSTAND YOUR OWN STRENGTH

(I FEEL)

A scientist once said: "If you could extract all the food strength from one peanut you would create enough energy to keep you going for an entire day".

Sounds unbelievable. But most of the things we once considered as idle dreams are today's realities.

A FACT IS A DREAM THAT HAS BEEN REALIZED BY THE WILL OF THE DREAMER.

So it is with your own strength. You never understand what it can do until you put to the test.

I do not mean your strength in the terms of the number of pounds you can raise over your head. No matter how strong a man may be, a small crane can easily out lift him.

By your strength, I mean your strength of Will. Your strength of purpose and your strength of faith.

I might call it your ability, for your strength lies in your willingness to adhere to your determination.

It is only by trying your strength that you will realize how much strength you have to call on. There is absolutely no limit to your strength. The Master shares His strength with you, just as He shares His wisdom with you. All the knowledge, strength and Power you will ever need to meet and overcome any problem is already yours. Don't look to others for help. Don't look to others for guidance. Look to the Master. Merely say, "Master, I am placing my problem in your hands. Help me do that which You wish me to do. I know that Your intentions for me are perfect intentions, for only your mind can conceive perfection."

Once you have placed your problem into the Hands of the Master let it stay there. Don't worry about it. Don't fret over it. Be assured that something will be done about it, all in good time. And you will be the person who will do the something about it. You will receive your instructions in the way all your instructions will come, that is in the silence. Trust the Master and follow His guidance when it comes.

In this way you can do no wrong. You must do the right thing, for you will be doing the Master's work.

There is a perfect way of testing your own strength. Give it work to do. Give it an object to attain. Your strength is only as potent as your faith. If your faith is boundless your strength will know no limits.

While your strength is yours to use in your own progress, it is not meant to be used for yourself alone. You are to divert some of your new-found Power to the benefit of others.

If your Power is true then it is meant to be used for the glory of the Master.

When you can walk and act by yourself, then the time has arrived when you can help others. You can put your strength to work in order to show and inspire others to what they themselves can do. For the things that you have attained are also possible to anyone who will possess the Will to attain.

The Master's gifts are for the entire world. They are always waiting to be used. They are not the exclusive property of any one man or any one group or groups of men. They belong to the world and to all the people of the world. They belong to the person who is willing to reach out for them.

By a steady practice of your strength and by a continued use of your Power you can show others what they can do.

You can also do more than merely show others what they themselves can do. You can at times actually do things for others.

The same concentration, the same application, the same faith that has given you the Power to stand on your own feet, alone, can always be diverted through the proper channels to help the world.

Color, creed, race or language must never be a barrier in your thoughts or in your work. We are all identical creations of the Master. In His mind and in His sight we are equal, one with the other. Color, creed, race or language are merely accidents of birth. They are the artificial barriers that foolish people have erected between themselves and their neighbors. They are merely instru ments and manifestations of fear, greed or envy.

These distinctions must never have a part in your thinking or in your actions. Man is brother to man. And the question, "Am I my brother's keeper?" has a significance that few are willing to face.

Never wish for that which another's. It may seem most tempting. You may even think that you need what another has. You may even persuade yourself that it is necessary to your own existence. Whatever it may be that another has, can be yours if you Will it, intelligently and sincerely. Whatever position another has attained can be yours, if you Will it and prepare for it. What man has already done, so you can do. What man has never yet accomplished you Can accomplish if your Will and your thoughts are strong enough to carry you to your goal.

Bear in mind that you must live in the today. Tomorrow is the day when you will profit by yesterday's examples. The Now is the important hour. It is the tool you hold in your hand for the work that you are doing at the moment.

It is only by understanding your own strength, by knowing that there is absolutely no limit to it when it flows through you from the Master, it is by knowing that your supply is unlimited, that it is there for you to call upon at all times, it is by truly knowing these things that your strength will be equal to any task that circumstances may set for it.

Then, and only then, will you come to the full realization of the Power of your own strength.

THE NINTH STEP

YOU LEARN HOW TO GIVE AND RECEIVE

(I KNOW)

This may well be the most important step in your progress.

The title in itself may sound simple. You may say, "Surely, everybody knows how to give and to receive." "Why waste any of my valuable time on something that is instinctive".

Before you read much further you will find that it is not as simple as you may believe. The person who can give and receive gracefully and thankfully is rare indeed.

With your new-found strength and Power you can make these two important acts as natural to your everyday life as breathing and sleeping.

You must learn to give thanks to the Master for the gifts and for the assistance you are about to receive. The mere fact that you ask for assistance should be ample proof that the assistance actually exists. The very act by which you call upon the Master should be sufficient proof to you that the Master is. You must assume that the assistant that you ask for is already in your hands when you ask for it.

In your world there is no lack of anything that you need. If you feel the need of anything, that which you require exists. You would not have need of something that does not exist. If it exists it is at the disposal of the Master. Since you are one with the Master, all things are yours. Think it over carefully. Know that the world is yours for the taking.

Never hesitate to give thanks for the things you have received, are about to receive or for the things you hope to receive.

Many people look upon giving thanks as a sign of weakness. They feel that it puts them in the position of humbling themselves before another. They feel that by giving thanks they are making themselves inferior. They imagine that their taking and their thankfulness will make them appear smaller in the sight of the giver.

This is wrong.

If you think that way, change your thinking.

That which is given to you comes not through the grace of any one individual. It comes to you direct from the Master who is aware of your need. The giver is merely the instrument through which the Master is working.

You are doing the work of the Master by graciously accepting and by giving thanks for all His gifts, even before you know what the gifts may be.

You must be as willing to give freely as you are to accept.

You must learn to give freely of the things that you may hold, be they thoughts or material things.

By the giving of your material possessions you are doing the Master's work. Nothing that you have is really yours. You hold it temporarily through the grace and the bounty of the Master. You are the momentary custodian. It is only by giving the things you have to another that makes these things your own.

The only things we really own are those things which we can give to others.

This applies to all things, wealth, knowledge or Power.

The wealth that we give to others is the only wealth we ever keep. The giving brings to us the thankfulness of the receiver. It is this thankfulness that adds another star to our Crown. These are the treasures that we lay up for ourselves. These are the treasures than no one can steal from us. These are the treasures that neither moth nor dust can corrupt. They are ours forever.

More and more of the wealth of the world come to us as we can demonstrate that we know how to use it wisely and to the glory of the Master.

Material wealth is merely another of the gifts of the Master. He gives it to us in abundance when He knows that we know how to use it.

I have gone into this demonstration in greater detail in my book, **"The magic formula for successful prayer"**. I do not wish to repeat myself; hence I refer you to that work.

Another form of giving that you should practice is the giving of good thoughts.

Maimonides, the famous Hebrew thinker, speaks of the charity of thought as being the greatest of the eight forms of charity.

By charity of thought you are taught to give your good thoughts to all. To the people you know, to those you do not know. For those that you do not know may know of your or you may get to know them at some later stage of your life. And since we are all brothers, creations of the on Master, it is only because of time and space that we are kept from the intimate knowledge of all our brothers.

Therefore think well of the entire world and its people. Their virtues you will engrave on the tablets of memory, their faults you will write on the sands.

At all times send good thoughts out upon the thought waves that circle the earth. They may find a welcome in the heart of some deserving soul who is hungering for the good thought of another.

Do not blame others for their errors. Think kindly of them for they know not what they do.

Help them by giving them the assistance and the comfort of your thoughts, your kind thoughts, your helpful thoughts. For thoughts can help another just as thoughts have helped you in your progress to your Power-aim.

You must learn to accept gracefully anything that is given to you. You must learn that by accepting what is offered you are actually helping another person to attain his destiny.

This goes for material things as well as spiritual. As your learn to accept you likewise learn to give. The two are linked together by an unbreakable bond.

If you have erred, learn to accept gracefully the fruits of your errors. Do not argue over the justice of the case, for in the Master's eyes true justice is always meted out in its true degree.

Be quick with your thanks whether it be to a brother or to the Master.

Do not be self-conscious or permit a false pride to overcome you. Honest thanks are at once your greatest duty and your highest privilege.

You owe nothing to the giver or his generosity. Often the giver is indebted to you for accepting his bounty. You have done him a service by your acceptance.

And when you give, do not give with conditions or strings tied to your gift.

Give freely, with the fullness of your heart and with the bounty of the Master.

And when you receive, accept with thankfulness in your heart. It was just another way in which the wishes of the Master have been manifested. You have been the instrument through which His will has been done.

When you give to others you are opening the way for more and greater blessings to be bestowed upon you. When you accept from others you are opening the channel through which greater and more permanent gifts may come to you.

Give with grace and freedom.

Accept with grace and thankfulness.

Do both with an open heart and know that it is the will of the Master.

Know that what you give is given through your own Power.

Know that what you accept comes to you to strengthen your own Power-aim.

THE TENTH STEP

POWER IS YOURS

(I AM)

At last you have arrived at that stage where you know that Power is yours.

Now you must make the best use of it.

It is your so long as you use it wisely and with understanding. That which you hoard becomes fool's gold and disappears with the first wind. The only things you keep are the things you give away.

You must continue to make your contacts with the Master with regularity. You must make your association with the Master a personal association.

Look upon him as a guide, as a friend, as a teacher, as a helper. Go to Him with every new problem when the problem comes into your life. Discuss every new situation with Him. Go to Him with courage and understanding. Go to Him with humility. Pride should have no place in your life.

You must not be proud of what you have learned or gained. You can lose either of these things much easier than you attained them. Pride should have no place in your life or in your thinking.

Pride cometh before the fall.

Keep your goal ever before you.

Now you have reached the stage where you must be prepared to advance your goal to a higher plane whenever that becomes necessary.

Someone once said that there were but two tragedies in life. One was in not getting the things you want, the other was in getting them. Of the two, the latter is infinitely the greater tragedy.

So it is with your goal. Once you attain it, you have no place to go. That is, no place but backwards, unless you have prepared for this emergency.

You are lost unless you have already moved your goal further ahead, still higher, so that you still have something to work for, so that you still have something to aim for, so that you still have something to strive for.

For man does not attain perfection in this life. That is one of the treasures that awaits us in the future. This life is merely a testing ground for the next.

But do not think that all his work, all this striving for your Power-aim has no point, no reason, if we are not to attain our Perfect goal.

It has a reason, it has an end; that end is to make us better people on this earth. To make us better neighbors, better friends, better parents, better children of the Master, so that through our striving for perfection we may help those whose lives touch ours in the enjoyment of the glories that our climb towards our Power-aim has revealed to us.

From time to time it will be wise to return to the earlier chapters of this book and use them as exercises to keep you in the perfect form that all artists maintain.

The world famous concert pianist will continually practice the scales, knowing that perfection in the simplest rudiments of his art will help to the perfection of the most difficult exercises.

So should it be with you. Since your ultimate aim is perfection in the way of living, your time should be divided between the practice of the simple elementary steps and in living the lessons that you have learned. In this way you will at all times be prepared for the exercises that demand your full strength, your full Power and your full perfection.

CONCLUSIONS

Conclusions seem a strange word to use as the title of this chapter. In every truth it should be called the Introduction. For these pages have merely been an Introduction to your labors in the attainment of your Power-aim.

How you progress depends entirely upon yourself. No one can help you. That is, no one but the Master. You must develop your own Will to Power. You must build up your own strength. You must promote your own ability to sit in the silence and hear the words of the Master make themselves clear in your mind, in your heart and in your inner-self.

It does not matter whether you take a year or a lifetime to attain your goal. Time is the most unimportant consideration in this quest.

While it is true that you read all the words in this book in a few hours, it will require infinite practice, great patience and supreme fortitude on your part to make these pages a part of your daily life.

You ask, "Will it be worth while?"

You are the only person who can answer that question for yourself. You know what you want out of life. You are a thinking person; otherwise you would never have started to read this book. You wanted to improve yourself, your circumstances, your surroundings, your thinking. You are, or should be the master of your own destiny.

I can tell you, from the many letter that I have received from the readers of my others books, that the quest is well worth while. These people have told me what these works did for them. They can do as much for you.

During the years I have had ample opportunity to observe the working of these laws. I have seen people grow. I have seen people, men and women alike, strive for their goal. I have seen the great happiness in their hearts. I have seen the great happiness in their hearts. I have seen them make their Power work for them to their greater glory, and I have seen them go onward and upward, firm in their conviction that their Power-aim is the way of their life.

I have sat in the silence and heard the small, still voice of the Master. I have the faith. Can you have less?

EXERCISES

FOR DEVELOPMENT...

FOR ATTAINMENT...

FOR PERFECTION...

The exercises of affirmations which follows are given to you as a tangible means of attaining the results for which they are meant.

To the person who "knows it all" they will be just words. But to you, who know and realize the Power of intelligently directed thought, they can be constant and faithful companions in your Power-demonstrations.

Words have a peculiar quality. They have an individuality just as humans. Words in themselves have no power to accomplish or attain. But the effect that certain words or combinations of words have upon our thinking or our actions is apparent to any one who has given this subject the serious thought it deserves.

Affirmations are in this class. In themselves they are just words. But the influence they exert on the person who sincerely says and means the affirmations, is beyond our power of logical and reasonable explanations.

I have seen many cases where the immediate action of these and similar affirmations have been little short of miraculous.

By a constant and intelligent use of these and similar affirmations you should be able to accomplish demonstrations to your own satisfaction.

The constant repetition of these words will so impress them on your consciousness that you will soon understand the reason for their use and Power of the sincerely spoken word.

You ask me, how, when and where you should use affirmations.

Use them in your sessions in the silence. Use them when doubt, fear, or confusion threatens to come into your consciousness. Use them when some obstacle appears in your path. Use them in moments of strength as well as in moments of weakness. Use them to attain the ends to which they specifically allude.

Make their inner meaning a part of your thinking. Have them ready when you need them. Use them as often as you wish, wherever you are and however you will.

They are yours to use. Yours to give to others who have need of their Power.

Make them a part of your life. They will demonstrate their ability to serve you under all circumstances.

IF YOU ARE SERIOUS IN YOUR EFFORT TO ATTAIN YOUR PERSONAL POWER-AIM I SUGGEST THAT YOU COMMIT THE FOLLOWING AFFIRMATIONS TO MEMORY.

AFFIRMATIONS
FOR HEALTH

The spirit of health, through the grace of the master, fills my mind and body.

I am continually renewed in body, mind, spirit and will through my oneness with the Master.

I am strengthened and healed by the power of the Master with me.

Knowing that my faith in the Master is my health and well being, I am tower of strength and faith.

I am the creation of the Master who made all things and pronounced them perfect. Therefore I am perfect in mind, body and spirit.

AFFIRMATIONS
FOR FORGIVENESS

Master, I understand that as I forgive others so will I be forgiven.

I see god in all men.

The Master's forgiveness working through me inspires me to be forgiving at all times.

The forgiving Master sets me free from all fear and I forgive all.

When things and persons of the world seem to disturb, I turn to the silent presence of the Master within me.

AFFIRMATIONS
FOR PROTECTION

My unlimited faith in the Master is my constant protection.

Wherever I am there also is the Master.

I rise above every thought of fear and doubt because I know the Master is always at my side.

The protecting presence of the Master is my constant protection wherever I am, wherever I go.

Neither sin or evil nor failure has power in my life because in truth there is only the Master.

AFFIRMATIONS FOR LOVE

The love that the Master showers upon me is mirrored in the love that I hold for those around me.

Through the love of the Master I am released from every unloving thought.

I am ever thankful because I realize I have much to be thankful for.

The love of the Master in my heart now controls my world and finds expression in my love for all.

I am inspired to be loving because of the love of the Master within me.

AFFIRMATIONS
FOR COURAGE

My strength, constantly renewed is a daily demonstration of my faith in the Master.

I am free from all fear for the courage of true understanding has made me free.

The power of the Master growing in my understanding releases me from thoughts of sin, evil, sickness and need.

I have perfect faith that through the Master within me I can do al things.

With the true understanding of freedom I know there is no bondage.

AFFIRMATIONS FOR FRIENDSHIP

The judgment of the Master manifesting itself through me inspires me to be at all times a friend to all.

I know that all men are my brothers and my friends.

Instead of finding fault I am glad to praise the good in all men.

The justice of the Master teaches me to be just to all, and in turn the world will be just to me.

The radiance of the Master shining through me illuminates my path and the lives of those around me.

AFFIRMATIONS OF CONFIDENCE

The Master working through me constantly inspires me to demonstrate his perfection through everything I do.

My faith in the Master daily fills me with renewed vigor and understanding.

As I understand the Master's truth so am I inspired to radiate truth.

Through the power of the Master working in my consciousness I have complete control over the affairs of my life.

The perfection of the Master proves to me my own perfection.

AFFIRMATIONS FOR PROSPERITY

Knowing that my supply of plenty is constantly replenished I am conscious of the Master's wisdom in the manner in which I will be increasingly supplied.

My will in tune with the Master increases my spiritual riches and abundance manifests itself in all my doings.

I cannot want for any of the world's substance as long as the Master's unlimited supply is at my disposal.

I am patient because I know the Master will manage and arrange all my affairs.

The laws of the Master control my actions and my affairs and they are in perfect harmony.

AFFIRMATIONS FOR WISDOM AND UNDERSTANDING

The wisdom of the perfect mind directs me at all times.

The all-embracing love of the Master will bring harmony and understanding to the people of the world.

I am constantly directed in all the things I do and my life is one of peace, understanding and abundance.

Through the power of the Master within me I have power over my life and doings.

The wisdom of the master directs my steps and my way is true.

AFFIRMATIONS FOR HAPPINESS

At one with the master we are governed by his inspired peace, harmony and love.

The peaceful presence of the Master fills me and I am at peace.

I know that all things are working together for my good for I can see the hand of the Master in all my affairs.

I live in the present knowledge that all blessings are mine now.

I cannot be separated from the Master. I am one with his blessings.

HOW TO OVERCOME PROBLEMS FOR YOURSELF AND OTHERS

To begin with, we must thoroughly understand that most of the problems that plague us are problems that we ourselves create.

It is simple to trace the cause or the birth of these problems. If we do so we find that they are the result of our fears, cowardice, false pride, lack of faith, weakness of will, lack of true understanding or some other equally obvious lack on our part.

When you have a problem that cries for solution, the first thing to do is to ask yourself, "Just what is this problem. How did it come into being?" Then think it out until you have the answers to these questions.

Then, understanding it completely, go into the silence. Ask the Master to give you courage and understanding. The very fact that you have a problem should be s demonstration that you, with the help of the Master, can solve it.

Never forget that the Master within is your unlimited Power to accomplish and attain all things.

No matter what your problem may be, whether it is financial, personal or one of health, place it sincerely into the hands of the Master. Once you have done this you must understand and feel that the problem is well on its way to being solved. His wisdom and His Will working through you will give you a demonstration of your ability to understand his guidance.

Most problems are given to you as a test of your faith. No one is given a greater load to bear than he can carry. Unless, of course, that individual purposely attracts problems to himself.

This is not black magic, but merely an extension of the thought, that we are what we think.

If a problem should enter your life know what it is within your power to meet it, otherwise it would never have been placed in your consciousness.

Let the Master work through you. You are His child. Go to Him with trust and faith. Do not doubt. Do not question. Your answer will be given to you.

Have faith in the Master in all things. He is the way.

A WORD FROM
THE AUTHOR

I am about to make a strange request.

After you have re-read this book and profited by its presentation of the basic laws for your approach to tour Power-aim, tell some friend about it.

Do this discretely, not in a boastful way, but as a suggestion as a means through which this friend might come to the way of the Master.

Do not lend them your copy of this book, but suggest that they own one, just as you do.

I say this for several reasons.

I want to keep this book and re-read it from time to time. You remember, I spoke of going to the basic lessons. None of us can reach that state of perfection where we can neglect the first steps in our approach to Power.

Your friend will surely want a copy, for this is not a book to read through hurriedly.

You can help spread this philosophy of faith, kindness and understanding.

You will actually be doing a good turn to your friend.

I will tell him that it comes through your bounty or not, as you prefer. A number of people have had me send my other books to their friends without mentioning their names. It is just another way of helping another soul find the way.

Mikhail Strabo

Notes:

ORDER FORM

Name				
Street and Number				
City, State and Zip Code				
Date of Birth:				
email:				

QTY:	ITEM #	BOOK DESCRIPTION	Price	Total
	71381	The 21 Divisions by Carlos Montenegro	$9.95	
	72254	The Book of Meditation	10.95	
	72299	Change your Life (Bilingual)	9.95	
	73574	The Book of Psalms	10.95	
	72244	Clairvoyance and Occult Powers	10.95	
	72294	Egyptian Magic	10.95	
	72295	Evil Eye	10.95	
	72296	Genuine Mediumnship	10.95	
	72298	God's Healing Gifts	9.95	
	70007	The Guiding Light to Power and Success	9.95	
	72256	Gypsy Sorcery and Fortune Telling	9.95	
	72243	How to Heal your Emotions	9.95	
	72257	The Magic Book of Money and Riches	10.95	

Shipping outside USA: $3.00 USD 1st book $2.00 USD each additional book.	SUB TOTAL:	
	FREE SHIPPING IF YOU LIVE IN THE USA!!!	
	8. If you live in California, add state tax: **8%**	
	9. GRAND TOTAL:	

To pay by Credit Card, write your information clearly:

1	2	3	4	5	6	7	8	9	10	11	12	13	14	15	16

☐☐ / ☐☐   ☐☐☐

Expiration Date   Security Code

Our terms are FOB shipping point. Your credit card will be charged until shipment.

Day phone number: _____-_____-_____

Name on Card: _____

Address: _____ Zip _____

Today's date: _____/_____/_____

Sign here: _____

PAYMENT FORM:
___Check
___Cash US Dlls.
___Money Order
___Credit Card
___Postage-Stamps

PRICES EXPIRE JAN 2020

Questions?
sales@myJaguarBooks.com
Phone: (714) 836-0627

FREE Catalog with your ORDER

SEND YOUR ORDER TO:
FAX 714-274-7199 OR TO:

JAGUAR BOOKS™

17645 Bobrick Ave, Lake Elsinore, CA 92530